The Fabian Society

The Fabian Society is Britain's leading left of cen
political society, committed to creating the politic
debates which can shape the future of progressive

With over 300 Fabian MPs, MEPs, Peers, MSPs and AMs, the Society
plays an unparalleled role in linking the ability to influence policy
debates at the highest level with vigorous grassroots debate among our
growing membership of over 7000 people, 70 local branches meeting
regularly throughout Britain and a vibrant Young Fabian section
organising its own activities. Fabian publications, events and ideas
therefore reach and influence a wider audience than those of any
comparable think tank. The Society is unique among think tanks in
being a thriving, democratically-constituted membership organisation,
affiliated to the Labour Party but organisationally and editorially
independent.

For over 120 years Fabians have been central to every important
renewal and revision of left of centre thinking. The Fabian commitment
to open and participatory debate is as important today as ever before
as we explore the ideas, politics and policies which will define the next
generation of progressive politics in Britain, Europe and around the
world. Find out more at **www.fabian-society.org.uk**

i

Fabian Society
11 Dartmouth Street
London SW1H 9BN
www.fabian-society.org.uk

Fabian ideas
Series editor: Jonathan Heawood

First published September 2004

ISBN 0 7163 0612 3
ISSN 1469 0136

British Library Cataloguing in Publication data.
A catalogue record for this book is available from the British Library.

Printed in Glasgow by Bell & Bain

Fabian Thinkers

120 years of progressive thought

edited by
Ellie Levenson
Guy Lodge
Greg Rosen

Acknowledgements

The editors would like to thank Adrian Harvey for his help and encouragement at the beginning of this project and all the members of the Fabian Research and Publications Committee for their ideas and suggestions during the planning stages, in particular Tony Wright MP, without whom this pamphlet would have taken a very different shape. They would also like to thank the Webb Memorial Trust, whose financial assistance made this publication possible.

Contents

This pamphlet is dedicated to
the memory of Ben Pimlott
1945-2004

Introduction
Sunder Katwala

Nobody can know exactly what George Bernard Shaw, HG Wells or Sidney and Beatrice Webb would make of the world of Tony Blair, low-cost airlines and the internet.

But then their Britain seems quite alien to us too. The Britain of 1884 was one in which most working men were denied the vote - along with all women - while wives were little more than the property of their husbands. The British Empire was at the height of its powers and its eclipse seemed unthinkable. The narrow political battle was between Gladstonian liberalism and Toryism. These must hardly have seemed auspicious circumstances for the small and idealistic group which met in solicitor Edward Pease's house in London to form the Fabian Society and declared their ambition to 'help in the reconstruction of society in accordance with the highest moral possibilities.'

Yet the Fabians were confident that their ideas could change the world. They were - though they would not have recognised the term - creating the world's first 'thinktank' and surely the most influential in the world of practical politics.

Armed with facts, arguments and political persuasion, the Fabians created a uniquely practical utopianism. It was not just that they were able to 'imagine things that never were and ask "why not"' (a Shaw soundbite later adopted by Bobby Kennedy). It was also that the Fabians educated and organised to make things happen in practice.

They were first to propose many influential ideas - a national medical service and a welfare state funded by progressive taxation, equal rights for women and decolonisation. In addition to their ideas, publications and lectures, they created a highly impressive institutional legacy to create pressure for these reforms. Fabians helped to create the Labour Party in 1900. Convinced of the need for evidence-based social science, the Webbs founded the London School of Economics, and set up the *New Statesman* to provide an outlet for political debate and ideas.

Are these achievements anything more than a historical curiosity today? The fame and enduring reputation of many of the early Fabians could, after all, prove a burden as well as an asset for a thriving contemporary thinktank and political society, which will naturally be judged on its ability to shape the political debates of today and tomorrow, not those of yesterday. The Fabian Society's central role is to lead debate in defining the future ideas, politics and policies of the left and to show that progressives can win the next battle of political ideas.

Yet, in doing so, we can take inspiration from our roots. After all, what is most striking about the early Fabians is not that they provide a roll call of many of the most eminent thinkers of the Victorian and Edwardian age - the Webbs, Shaw, HG Wells, Rupert Brooke, Emmeline Pankhurst and many more - but the extent to which they were prepared to think ahead of the seemingly immutable features of the politics and society of their own times.

Most importantly, they demonstrated that ideas matter in politics. The impact of ideas is often disguised and understated. After all, ideas, however revolutionary when proposed, quickly become part of the political furniture. Yet it is often the battle of ideas, with its revolutions and counter-revolutions, which reshapes the boundaries of what is politically possible at any given time. And it is the ability of governments not just to legislate for their programmes but to shift their political opponents onto new territory which defines a lasting political legacy.

Few today, especially on the left, would share the early Fabians' characteristically Victorian certainty in 'the inevitability of gradualness'. Rather, today it is common for neo-conservatives and neo-liberals to believe that history is preordained to go their way. Yet this too is disingenuous. Ideas need political champions to succeed. Richard Cockett's definitive book, *Thinking the Unthinkable*, on the rise of the 'new right' (a label first applied by a Fabian critique) shows how the neo-liberal movement was explicitly modelled on the influence of Fabianism, which it sought to emulate, and counter, through institutions such as the Institute of Economic Affairs.

For political ideas to be effective, they must be constantly rethought. A good Fabian slogan might be 'revisionists revise'. The Fabian ability to influence across political generations has been achieved through the plurality and diversity of Fabian thinking - a constant rethinking for every political generation of what it means to be progressive and on the left. Every time there has been an important renewal of left-of-centre thinking, Fabians have been central to the debate.

Thus Sidney Webb wrote the Labour Party's constitution in 1918, including the famous clause four commitment to nationalisation, and Fabians played a central role in the debates which led to the Labour party rewriting its statement of aims and values in 1995 as it sought to escape its years in the electoral wilderness, particularly through Giles Radice's highly influential *Southern Discomfort* pamphlets which asked what stopped voters disenchanted with the Conservatives switching to Labour. And the time has come to renew again - we must re-examine the founding myths and fears of New Labour as we seek to ensure a radical third Labour term.

As the 12 essays in this collection show, disagreement and debate is built into the fabric of the Fabian approach - underpinned by the lack of any collective Fabian 'line' on policy issues. The ideal of open-minded, rational disagreement has not always been achieved in practice - HG Wells stormed out of the Society and lampooned the Webbs in his satire *The New Machiavelli* while the formation of the SDP created deep divisions a generation ago. And few would claim that Fabians have got everything right - the early Fabian claim that markets were inefficient simply by virtue of being unplanned was clearly a mistake, and the Webbs in particular have been much criticised for their grey statist approach and their naivety, late in life, about the Soviet Union.

But many of the most telling critiques have come from within the Fabian fold, such as Anthony Crosland's famous claim in *The Future of Socialism* - easily the most influential book for the postwar left - that 'total abstinence and a good filing system are not now the right signposts to the socialist Utopia.' Conversely, Crosland's call for a greater emphasis on 'freedom and dissent, on culture, beauty, leisure, and even frivolity' still stands among the most eloquent expressions of an attractive ethical, democratic and participatory vision of what it is to be on the left. The values and ideas of William Morris, RH Tawney, GDH Cole and many others can similarly still influence contemporary political debates.

A long Fabian history has inevitably contained low as well as high points - the Society's non-sectarian approach was somewhat out of step with the political mood of both the 1930s and the 1970s. Yet we Fabians enter our thirteenth decade in particularly good health. Two Labour landslides have seen more Fabians returned to the House of Commons than Conservatives and Liberal Democrat MPs put together - their number including Stephen Twigg whose shock defeat of Michael Portillo on election night in 1997 meant he had to give up his post as Fabian general secretary.

Today, the membership of the Society is twice what it was 30 years ago and stands at its highest level since Clement Attlee was Prime Minister. While under previous Labour governments Fabian membership has fallen, it has continued to rise steadily each year since 1997 - just one sign that, for all of the talk of apathy, there is immense interest in politics today, though increasingly often this is taking place outside formal party political structures.

The great questions which will shape the next era of political debate - revitalising democracy and political participation; reshaping the relationship between citizens and the state; making environmentalism central to mainstream politics and creating an effective internationalism which can hold power to account in a global age - will require new and innovative thinking to create a progressive politics for our own age.

Yet the early Fabians would still find much that was recognisable in our contributions to these debates. The traditions of gradualism remain strong - especially the tactic of breaking political taboos to open up new ground in debates, as with our influential Commissions on Taxation and on the Monarchy. Our Life Chances Commission, launched in early 2004, will set out a road-map for the Labour Government's ambitious goal of abolishing child poverty by 2020. It returns to a perennial Fabian theme of social justice, and indeed contains echoes of the Society's very first pamphlet, *Why Are the Many Poor?*

Whether they would be, on balance, more encouraged or dismayed by the condition of contemporary Britain, those who founded the Fabian Society in 1884 would perhaps be surprised to find it still going strong 120 years on. In his essay, 'Sixty Years of Fabianism', George Bernard Shaw, then aged 90, concluded that he must 'retire to make room for the Fabians of 60 years hence, by whatever name they will then be called. For the name may perish, but not the species.' We can do no more than commend his thought to the Fabians of 2064.

1 | Annie Besant 1847-1933
Yasmin Khan

In India there are parks and roads named after Annie Besant, and she frequently makes an appearance in history textbooks. She is remembered there for her work in the twentieth century: the presidency of the Indian National Congress, her advocacy of independence for Indians and her leadership of the Theosophical Society. But in her native country, she is not so well recognised. This is typical of Besant who was always good at making herself unpopular in Britain. Her ideological U-turns - from Christianity to freethought and from socialism to theosophy - stunned even her admirers, and leave it difficult to associate her with any one movement or cause.

Yet she was on the frontline of British politics for some 25 years before moving to India, and was for George Bernard Shaw 'the greatest orator in England' at the time when she joined the Fabian Society in 1885. It was the second year of the Society's existence; it had fewer than 40 members and the middle-aged and bullish Besant, who always preferred to be the leader of any group, and was more comfortable with direct action than political philosophy, did not find a natural home there. Later she claimed that she only joined the Fabians because it was more palatable to her old radical friends than the other socialist groups. It is testimony to the lack of dogma and orthodoxy in the organisation (characteristic of the Fabian Society as a whole) that Besant started lecturing and publishing under the Fabian banner. But she also had some utility for the Fabians: she was an accomplished publicist and organiser (it was Besant who suggested the idea of local Fabian branches) and did not mind getting her hands dirty. Her energetic publicity work ensured that the 1889 *Fabian Essays in Socialism* sold like hot cakes.

Above all, she excelled at talking to ordinary people. Hubert Bland commented that she probably knew the views of the working classes better than all the other leading socialists of her day put together. It is this freshness and directness of description, rather than her philosophical insight, that speaks most loudly and clearly to us today. She was driven by a fiery humanitarianism, which never became detached in her mind from the effects of poverty. In her tract *Is Socialism Sound?* she stated baldly: 'The chief fact it deals with is the fact of poverty.' She was able to convey the effects of an unbridled capitalist system on the vulnerable - 'the sobs of women poisoned in lead works, exhausted in nail works, driven to prostitution by starvation, made old and haggard by ceaseless work' - and her journalism helped to underscore the importance of Fabian political thought.

Perhaps more than any other Fabian at the time, her principles of equality were not reserved for people in Britain. Her vision was international, and as she explained in *Why I am a Socialist*, it was because socialism was opposed to political, social and religious tyranny in every land, looked sympathetically at all nations struggling for their freedom and did not recognise barriers of nationality, class or creed that she was attracted to it. At a time of high empire, when other Fabians were ambivalent about the imperial project, Besant connected her domestic agenda with an international outlook which valued not only economic justice but also political freedom. In her eyes, the value placed on a life in Kabul or Mombassa ought to be exactly the same as that placed on a life in Bloomsbury. In fact she went beyond this, and her reading of international history was a subtle (if romanticised) critique of the ways in which the industrialised European countries had inhibited the development of the colonised parts of the world and distorted their political trajectories. Then as now, the problem was how to design policies to equalise life chances around the world, not only in Britain. As we grope for a response to the changing nature of the world order, there is a case to be made for bringing this humanitarian angle back into the rhetoric of policy formulation, even if the difficulties seem as insurmountable now as they did in 1885.

As a divorcee and single mother, with no other source of income, Besant supported herself entirely through lecturing and journalism. Her feminism was not spelt out. It was a basic assumption that underpinned everything else that she did. She mocked 'silly sneers at women's ability' and it was no wonder that she sat at Fabian meetings surrounded by young girls who hung on her every word. For her, feminism was not only for her middle class circle; she was just as interested in economic as political liberation for women. Her most famous victory was leading a union of factory girls against the match company Bryant and May and she was also involved in defending birth control. She resolved the apparent tension between the good of the community (including the family) and the good of the individual, which has sometimes undermined the place of feminism in socialism, by pointing to the social benefits of freeing women from economic hardship and rewarding them for their labour. She counted housework and child-care as part and parcel of this labour, anticipating the Women's Fabian Group by over 20 years. Her emphasis on the necessity of bringing the benefits of education and economic emancipation to all classes and ages of women is as relevant as ever.

Some may question Besant's suitability for inclusion in a pamphlet of this title, as she is more renowned for what she did than what she thought. She was indeed an activist rather than a thinker. It is not too paradoxical to say, though, that this frenetic and committed activity can speak to us still. She would have given apathetic voters short shrift. For her, politics was always something vital and exciting, and she felt a pressing responsibility to communicate this to the ordinary man and woman.

2 | George Bernard Shaw 1856-1950
Robin Cook

George Bernard Shaw's political writing had a profound impact on me as a teenager, and four decades later I am conscious of a personal debt to him. I still retain the beard I first grew in a spirit of emulation, even if it became a miniaturised version of his luxuriant growth when an election agent instructed me to cut it on the maxim, 'More hair: fewer votes'.

Shaw's distinctive contribution to the Fabian ethos was to humanise it. He parted from Marx over the determinist character of the doctrine of historical inevitability, which wrote free will out of the script as effectively as Calvinism. For Shaw, socialism could only be achieved by human will and conscious effort. His key commitment was to the power of reason, and he therefore believed that socialism must be built by persuasion, by argument and by deliberate choice.

The consequence was that he became the most active proselytiser among the early Fabians. In the decade after the formation of the Fabian Society he addressed 1000 meetings - in trade councils, Working Men's Clubs and debating societies, in every environment from open air parks to smoke-filled bars. Many of his earliest plays were written on trains and trams travelling to and from these engagements.

The motivation for this extraordinary campaigning output was in part a powerful anger at the injustice of Victorian society, but in part also a dramatist's enjoyment of performance. By all accounts the combination of his intellect and sense of drama was compelling. Annie Besant, the prototype feminist, was engaged to debate against Shaw, but after hearing his speech rose to announce her conversion to Fabianism.

Perhaps one of the aspects of Shaw that attracted her was his stout and outspoken advocacy of women's rights. His plays are replete with confident, assertive women who share his rejection of the injustice of 'saddling the right to a child with the obligation to become a servant of a man.' Emmeline Pankhurst confided that the character of Ann Whitefield in *Man and Superman* had 'strengthened her purpose and fortified her courage'. In his last political work, Shaw asserted that Parliament could only properly be called a House of Commons when men and women were represented in equal numbers, a goal that half a century later still eludes us.

Another Shavian theme that speaks to our time is his disgust at the stupidity and barbarity of war. Shaw was one of the first to point out that 'the mechanisation of modern war greatly reduces the power of human conscience' and that as a result, a youth of ordinary good nature 'will release a bomb that will blow a whole street of family homes into smithereens, burning, blinding, mutilating scores of mothers and babies, without seeing anything of his handiwork.' If he were alive today, Shaw would have exposed the moral contrast between our emotional response to the appalling decapitation of a single person with a knife and the relative indifference of our media to the killing of 10,000 Iraqis by bomb and missile.

Shaw's polemic on the folly of the British government in participating in the Great War was so magnificent that it immediately made him the target of patriots on the home front. His books were removed from libraries, his plays from the West End and the son of Prime Minister Asquith called for him to be shot. True to its long tradition of liberal vacillation the *Guardian* refused to publish a letter from him because 'one's duty now is to encourage and unite people'. Shaw's response to these critics was an uncompromising call to the soldiers of both armies to 'shoot their officers and go home'.

It was supreme confidence in his intellectual superiority that sustained Shaw in persisting in his views against all comers. This was a source of strength that made him an iconoclastic figure, enthusiastic about challenging convention and orthodoxy in a way that would rapidly have produced his expulsion from New Labour. The quintessential Shaw quotation is the one which celebrates the revolutionary power of original thought: 'The reasonable man adapts himself to the world: the unreasonable one persists in trying to adapt the world to himself. Therefore all progress depends on the unreasonable man.'

Yet over-confidence can also be a source of weakness. Shaw's fixation on the pioneering role of the intellectual contributed to his unhealthy tendency to attach too much importance to heroic leadership. This led him into the trap of naïve admiration for the top-down modernisation of Russia under the leadership of the Bolsheviks, which is a cause of embarrassment to even the most devoted Shavian. Its sole redeeming feature is that Stalin left their two hour meeting complaining that Shaw was an awful person.

Fortunately for Fabianism, Shaw had a much better grasp from first hand knowledge of the condition of working people in Britain. The result was a body of drama and tracts that to this day is unrivalled for its acute and biting account of an economic system that exposed the majority of the population to ruthless exploitation. Ironically it is not the intellectual analysis of which Shaw was so proud that makes his writing still resonate with us today, but his powerful moral indignation. In *Mrs Warren's Profession*, prostitution is only a metaphor for the experience of a proletarian class exploited by a bourgeoisie who owed their respectable place in society to a financial system that to Shaw was equally immoral.

Nor has Fabianism ever boasted another pamphleteer of such mordant wit. Shaw was a contemporary of Oscar Wilde and although his output had a more serious purpose, he could produce repartee just as sharp. On his ninetieth birthday he was interviewed by a young journalist who took his leave by expressing the hope that he would be able to interview Shaw when he was 100. With characteristic self-confidence Shaw replied: 'I don't see why not. You look healthy enough.'

11

3 | Beatrice Webb 1858-1943 and Sidney Webb 1859-1947
Guy Lodge

Beatrice and Sidney Webb formed the bedrock of Fabian thinking for over 30 years and along with the Old Gang of early Fabians they succeeded in changing the world they lived in. Like all 'big' thinkers, the Webbs can claim to have been ahead of their time. Sidney argued in favour of Lords reform in 1914, called for a national minimum wage in 1918 and predicted a customs union for Europe in 1923, while Beatrice vigorously argued in favour of equal pay between men and women.

At a more theoretical level, the Webbs taught us the importance of understanding the architecture of power. Unlike most of their contemporaries, who saw the state as a passive instrument that would deliver the socialist frontier, the Webbs recognised the need to develop a theory of the state. They were among the first to examine the structural form that socialism should take and to ask how this should interact with its citizenry. And it should be remembered that when they wrote about the state they were as likely to be talking about Wakefield local authority as Whitehall.

But the central ideas promulgated by the patron saints of collectivism seem unsuited for today's challenges. Public ownership and top-down economic planning have ceased to resonate as viable policy solutions, while the Webbs' migration to Soviet Communism has cast a shadow over their reputation. So it is perhaps unfortunate, though a testament to their Herculean effort, that Fabianism has come to be so heavily identified with the Webbs and their socialism, which was built on paternalistic, statist and technocratic foundations and operationalised through a bossy know-all bureaucracy. Though a caricature, and at times a misleading one - they were genuinely concerned about checking the excesses of state power and acknowledged the limitations that arise from government by elites - it nonetheless epitomises their outdated outlook.

The Webbs' lack of personal appeal and charisma is striking. They do not inspire or excite in the way that GDH Cole and Shaw do. This is the couple who used their honeymoon in Dublin to investigate Irish trade unionism. Beatrice, though fascinating, possessed a puritanical streak that is an instant turn-off. The self-confessed 'anti-flesh-fish-egg-alcohol-coffee-and-sugar-eater' would have made her presence felt in our current public health debates. One suspects that she would have had us all waking up to exercise drills. It is also questionable whether their work has stood the test of time. We do not cherish what Beatrice herself described as 'solid but unreadable books' in the way that we do Tawney's *Equality* or Crosland's *The Future of Socialism*. Ironically, it is Beatrice's diaries with which we are most familiar today. They offer a rare insight into the more human side of this intriguing couple. Nonetheless, the Webbs remain, in Shaw's phrase, 'unsocial socialists', and they were often guilty of thinking too much about administrative systems, conspicuously forgetting about the people whose lives such systems were designed to improve.

Yet when Crosland famously derided the Webbs, writing, 'total abstinence and a good filing system are not now the right signposts to the socialist utopia', he was only half right. The filing system was more important than Crosland acknowledged. Within it we find the enduring legacy of the Webbs - their distinct approach to politics, an approach that has been emulated ever since and remains acutely relevant today.

More than anyone else, it was the Webbs who established the Fabian tradition of conducting painstaking research and inquiry to solve the social and economic riddles thrown up by society. They pioneered the methodology of British socialism. While others would look to grand theories, Sidney would declare, 'here are the facts', and it was the facts underpinning their ideas which helped them defeat their intellectual adversaries of Marxism and laissez-faire individualism, ushering in a democratic collectivist era. It was a pragmatic and technocratic approach, but one that delivered. Political change, Beatrice wrote, would 'not be brought about through shouting but through hard thinking.'

Through their work, the Webbs developed and created a new school of economic and social science, founding the disciplines of social policy and public administration which now furnish today's policy community with expertise. The LSE, with its distinctly Webbian motto, *rerum cognoscere causas* - 'to understand the causes of things' - is a living monument to their way of doing things. For the Webbs, the pursuit of ideas was a functional exercise. They did not live in ivory towers. They were practical reformers intent on achieving progress. This explains why they did not just design the administrative fabric of the early twentieth century state, but were intimately involved in implementing it. Sidney was active on the London County Council (LCC) and a Cabinet member in the MacDonald Governments, while Beatrice's input into Royal Commissions and her work on poverty in London's East End played an invaluable role in addressing the 'Social Question' prevalent at the turn of the century. The Webbs were prolific agitators, educators and campaigners, who combined intellectual rigour with an unrivalled reformist instinct. It is these distinctive characteristics which make them stand out and which have contributed to their reputation.

Though they would have held the rise of the 'op-eders' and our highly opinionated political discourse with some disdain, they would not have felt out of place in today's evidence-based policy environment. In an age relatively absent of ideology and dogma, the Webbs would have flourished, celebrating the maxim, 'what matters is what works'. It might be said of modern governance that 'we are all managers now', an approach which (whether desirable or not) owes much to the influence of the Webbian tradition. At the end of the nineteenth century the Webbs were responding to the inefficiencies of unfettered capitalism. It was a time of immense change, analogous to our own turbulent period. It is during such times that the need for cogent dispassionate analysis is greatest. Today we need our own Webbs to step forward and make sense of our intensely complex world.

Ultimately, the Webbs teach us how to win political arguments. Yes they lacked the imagination and passion of thinkers such as William Morris, but this was a conscious decision. The Webbs rejected fantasy socialism; they were bland bureaucrats dedicated to achieving social improvement. But they succeeded where the more visionary and romantic failed. They radiated self-confidence, knowing that their ideas were the best out there. Crucially, they linked socialism with common sense. Sidney wrote that 'socialism is not a faith in an artificial utopia but a spreading conviction', and the Webbs were in the lead spreading that conviction persuasively and thoroughly. They did not couch their arguments in terms of building a New Jerusalem but instead spoke about delivering schools and hospitals efficiently. They were preaching to the unconverted. In doing so they entrenched their ideas in the political terrain, establishing the terms of reference with which others had to engage. It should be remembered that the Webbs were not rejected, but revised. Turning to Beatrice, in anticipation of losing his seat on the LCC, Sidney remarked: 'Most of my work they can't undo even if I am turned out.' The challenge currently facing us is how to cement our own agenda over those of our rivals, defining the political landscape on which they have to compete.

Today many of us crave a more profound narrative for the left. We want to be able to describe what the final destination will look like. Yet the harsh truth is that progress happens piecemeal, and while it can at times feel disappointing, it is often the way to get things done. Though the Webbs seem in so many respects a spent and even antiquated force in the history of the left, their enduring legacy remains a practical one. This, no doubt would have brought a smile (albeit a small and unassuming one) to their faces.

4 | HG Wells 1866-1946
Roy Hattersley

At first the Fabians believed that HG Wells was the answer to their secular prayers. *Anticipations* - now rightly regarded as a novel of little merit - was described by Beatrice Webb as 'the most remarkable book of the year.' It was Wells's first attempt to describe, in fiction, his vision of an ideal society. And, since it was the description of 'a series of collectives run by a managerial elite', it was the sort of utopia in which Fabians would have felt at home. But Wells turned out to be a difficult colleague.

Perhaps the Webbs should have realised, from the start, that they would not find Wells a soulmate. Edward Pease, the real founder of the Fabian Society, welcomed the new recruit as a rival rather than a complement to the intellectual inspirations of the movement. 'We have lived for years on the Webbs' new ideas of politics', he said. 'We want somebody else who can think ahead.' Wells thought ahead in a way which both reinvigorated and split the society.

The dispute between Wells and the Webbs was fundamental. It was set out in the memorial essay which Wells published after Beatrice's death in 1943: 'She went down to the poor as saints do. I came up from the poor in a state of flaming rebellion, most blasphemous and ungainly. Beatrice wanted to socialise the ruling classes and make them do their duty. I wanted to destroy them.'

When Wells joined the society, its formula for changing the world was the infiltration and conversion of other organisations. Wells, although a happy member of the intellectual elite, was also a class warrior. He believed that socialism - or at least his novel definition of that philosophy - must stand on its own feet, and he was particularly sceptical about hopes of using the Liberals as a vehicle for social reform. They were, in his view, 'not so much a party as a multitudinous assembly.' It was a strange criticism to come from a man who saw a close intellectual connection between socialism and cycling.

Wells's real complaint was that Fabians waited so long to strike hard that they ended up not striking at all. He wanted to create the New Jerusalem overnight. When he published *In The Days of the Comet* - the description of how a utopia of free love was created by a trail of gas which followed the ball of fire - George Bernard Shaw told him: 'You want to play the part of the comet.' There is no doubt that Wells had a high regard for his role in the transformation of society. But he regarded himself more as a teacher than an active revolutionary. He wanted to point the way to barricades which others would storm.

Many of the lessons were embodied in his books. Michael Foot's biography of Wells reminds us that 'all his heroes and most of his heroines called themselves socialists.' But it was not so much the beliefs of his characters as the descriptions of the society in which they lived which acted as propaganda for the cause. *Tono-Bungay* - named after the patent medicine which was no more than 'nothing coated in advertisements' - was a polemic against commercialism. *The War in the Air* denounced 'Europe all at sixes and sevens, with our silly flags and our silly newspapers raggin' us up against each other.' *A Modern Utopia*, set in a world of collective ownership, social welfare and industrial efficiency, was described as 'tracts turned into fiction.' *The New Machiavelli* was the story of a man who rose from humble beginnings to great fame and fortune but, because of a scandal involving a woman, was rejected by those he tried to help. It was not, therefore, wholly autobiographical. Wells's numerous scandalous relationships with women never harmed his career.

Wells wrote *The New Machiavelli* during his long and bitter parting from the Fabian Society. The implication that he had been treated badly - for any reason - was wholly misplaced. He had attacked it for years, describing the Webbs as advocating the socialism of the 'district visitor' and assuring Ford Maddox Ford that he was 'going to turn the society inside out and throw it in the dustbin.' Initially, he tried to change it from the inside by proposing a new constitution - the executive replaced by a council of 25 members which supervised three triumvirates which took responsibility for propaganda, membership and publicity. But his real objective was to change its policy, not its organisation.

He wanted to change the name of the Fabian Society to The British Socialist Society, mount a nationwide recruitment drive and run candidates for parliament. His aim was an end to what the Webbs called 'permeation' - the belief that the job of gradualists was to convince existing political organisations of the need to ameliorate the harshness of society. Wells wanted to build a new world. There were other incidents and excuses which he used to justify the split. Quite unreasonably he claimed that he could not remain in a society which published Shaw's *Fabians and the Fiscal Question*, the socialist case for protectionism. But his real problem with the Fabians stemmed from his particular view of the good life.

Wells was a scientist - both by training and instinct. What was more, he was a disciple of TH Huxley, 'Darwin's bulldog'. But his view of evolution was more pessimistic than the survival of the fittest. The species would, he feared, mutate until it destroyed itself - unless scientists of good will found a way of securing mankind's future by breeding a superior human race.

Anticipations and *A Modern Utopia* were both explicit about the need for population control - though Wells's critics and admirers have always argued with each other about how he proposed it should be brought about. His enemies cried 'eugenics' and claimed he wanted to eliminate inferior races. His supporters - citing *Ann Veronica* in evidence - insist that he had a view of reproduction which, since it proposed to limit the birth rate by freely available contraception, was the gospel of female liberation.

The Fabians believed - and perhaps they were right - that HG Wells, despite the turmoil which he created within the society, added a glitter to their activities because of his intellectual sparkle and social status as a controversial novelist. He also acted as a straightforward propagandist. *This Misery of Boots* began life as a lecture and became a pamphlet which satirised the class system with a virulence which made it the model of Fabian polemics for years to come. In *Socialism and the Middle Classes*, he attacked 'bourgeois marriage' and suggested that the state should take responsibility for the upbringing of children, thus releasing mothers from bondage.

Although Wells believed that his ideas were ahead of his time, his views on the family - free love, only the reproduction of the talented to be encouraged and 'state endowed' motherhood - seem as bizarre today as they did in Edwardian England. But they contained the germs of essential socialist ideas - not the least of which was the equality of the sexes. So the Fabians were right to regret losing him, despite the disruption that he caused. The Society was not ready for what Beatrice Webb called 'conversion into a Committee of Public Safety' and Wells was not willing to wait for the new dawn of socialism to come by gradual conversion. But he never lost faith. In 1922 and 1923 he stood as a Labour parliamentary candidate. He died a year after the end of the Second World War which he had so often predicted, and just as the socialist government, for which he longed, had begun to take its first hesitant steps towards utopia.

5 | RH Tawney 1880-1962
Raymond Plant

There can be little doubt that RH Tawney is the individual who has exercised the greatest degree of moral authority over the Labour Party and the wider Labour Movement in the UK. This is the result partly no doubt of his striking personality and its effect on his contemporaries, but for subsequent generations it has depended upon the intellectual and moral force of his books, particularly *Equality*, *The Acquisitive Society* and *Religion and the Rise of Capitalism*. Of these, the book on equality is the one which has perhaps had the most pervasive effect.

RH Tawney was born in 1880 and educated at Rugby and Balliol College Oxford. After graduation he went to live and work at Toynbee Hall in the East End of London, then as now a considerable agent for community development in that area. He then worked for the Children's Country Holiday Fund for three years. He subsequently became a lecturer in economics at Glasgow University and was also active in the Workers' Educational Association (WEA) a link which was to last for the rest of his life, and through which he exercised great influence.

Tawney enlisted during the First World War but refused a commission although he was eventually made a sergeant. He was badly wounded in 1916 and came back to the UK to work as a temporary civil servant and to continue with the WEA. In 1920 he joined the staff of the London School of Economics, becoming Reader and subsequently Professor of Economic History. His first book, *Religion and the Rise of*

Capitalism, was published in 1926. This book was both a study of the relationship between the rise of capitalism and Protestant forms of Christianity - issues which were central to Marx's historical materialism and to Max Weber's *The Protestant Ethic and the Spirit of Capitalism* - and also an embodiment of Tawney's own deeply held Christian beliefs, which were central to his conception of socialism.

For Tawney, the idea of a common good, which he saw as central to Christianity, was also crucial for socialism and indeed provided an interpretation of other political principles such as freedom, rights, the role of the state, community or fellowship and the relation of commerce to social purpose. The idea that there is a common good or social purpose to be found is central to Tawney's idea of socialism and the common good resides in that set of conditions which can enable each individual who has dignity and worth as a human being to develop himself or herself and to 'perfect their condition,' as he put it in *Equality*. Central to the idea of the common good was the notion of purpose or function: in order for us to perfect ourselves we need to fulfil a function that achieves or reflects some social purpose. Tawney made this a central theme in *The Acquisitive Society*. In his view, the idea of a common good had become eroded in a rampantly capitalist society, and industry and commerce, instead of being geared to the achievement of this common good and the perfection of the condition of individuals, were now seen more or less as an end in themselves. At the same time, capitalism had exacerbated inequality in terms of both the basic dignity and worth of individuals and the levels of material inequality which made it impossible to see how some individuals would ever make the best of themselves. In Tawney's view, a central task of a socialist society was to ensure that business and commerce should serve social purposes and be constrained by a conception of the common good.

The idea of the common good also has a significant impact on Tawney's views on the nature of freedom and rights. While Tawney did not reject the idea of negative liberty - to be free from coercion - he did argue that we have to be concerned with the conditions of its exercise.

Otherwise, as he famously said, 'freedom for the pike is death for the minnows.' There had to be limitations on the degree of inequality in order for negative freedom to be effective. He also wanted to extend the concept of freedom to encompass the more positive view that, as he argues in *Equality*, 'a large measure of equality, far from being inimical to liberty, is essential to it.'

Similar considerations apply to rights. Individuals' rights should serve social purposes and functions: the perfection of the individual or the realisation of individual potential. This meant that rights were not absolute but had to be tested to see whether they fulfilled this function. It also meant that rights were not to be seen as negative rights - that is to say, the right to be left alone and not interfered with. So, for example, property rights were to be understood not in terms of the protection from interference of the existing pattern of property ownership, but in terms of the wider dispersal of property in society, so that individuals could use such property to achieve their potential. In *The Acquisitive Society* he argues that socialists must realise that 'the free disposal of a sufficiency of personal possessions is the condition of a healthy and self respecting life', and will therefore 'seek to distribute more widely the property rights which make them today the privilege of a minority.'

So, for Tawney, equality, freedom, rights and the common good go together. The common good is not something that stands over against individuals but is rather the common set of conditions, including forms of freedom, types of rights and limitations on the extent of inequality, which will secure to individuals what is necessary to them in respect of their basic moral standing and to enable them to realise their own distinctive powers and capacities as people.

Tawney did not believe in absolute equality of outcome. What he did think was important was the idea that there is this set of conditions necessary as basic goods which we all have in common and to which access should be as equal as we can make it. This for Tawney has more to do with what he calls equality of the environment, access to education, the means of civilisation, security and independence and 'the social consideration which equality in these matters usually comes with.' The achievement of this set of common and equal standards of citizenship and the recognition that we all need them and should all have equality of access to them would create a common sense of citizenship, a common sense of purpose and what he calls fellowship. This is a conception which many on the left in politics still share and which is still their inspiration.

6 | GDH Cole 1889-1959 and Margaret Cole 1893-1980
Tony Wright

The Coles, like the Webbs, belong to an era when partnerships lasted. This immediately makes them seem old-fashioned. In other respects, though, what they had to say seems strikingly contemporary. Douglas (always GDH) Cole and Margaret Postgate came together in the second decade of the twentieth century as young turks in the guild socialist 'movement' - as they liked to describe it - which was challenging the orthodoxies of Fabian collectivism in the name of a socialism that was decentralist, pluralist and self-governing.

For a time this new creed seemed to carry all before it, until the harsher political and economic climate of the interwar years closed down the space in which such ideas could flourish. The Coles therefore turned their prodigious energies to a whole range of intellectual and political activities that the needs of the time dictated (so numerous were their books that one reviewer suggested that they must be written by a syndicate); but they always remained, at bottom, the guild socialists of their youth. When Margaret, then in her seventies, climbed onto the pillion of my motorcycle at Oxford station some 30 years ago, it was to tell me about the enduring importance of the 'movement', and of her late husband's ideas.

GDH Cole did not invent guild socialism, but he soon became its leading intellectual exponent. Its core idea, forged in the climate of industrial turmoil that marked the first decade of the twentieth century, was for a form of workers' control, an assumption of responsibility by trade unions that recaptured the spirit of the medieval guilds but converted this into modern terms. To the young Cole, converted to socialism by a schoolboy reading of William Morris, this promised a version of socialism that was more appealing than the drab bureaucracy of the Webbs. Above all, it grasped the central point that the fundamental evil was not poverty but slavery, which could only be remedied by a doctrine of freedom and responsibility. In other words, people had to take control of their own lives, which neither capitalism nor collectivism allowed. 'In the state of today', wrote Cole in his *Self-Government in Industry*, 'in which democratic control through Parliament is little better than a farce, the Collectivist State would be the Earthly Paradise of bureaucracy.'

This was heady stuff. It was a deliberate challenge by the Coles to the Webbs and a clarion call to a new generation on the left. The decade or so which had the first world war in the middle was a period of extraordinary vitality in progressive social thinking in Britain, and guild socialism contributed much to this. By combining the academic assault on the state by the pluralists with the industrial assault on capitalism by the trade unions, GDH Cole in particular constructed an exciting and innovative synthesis. Starting with the world of labour, he produced a general social theory of self-government with ever more elaborate sketches of how such a world would actually work. It was a world in which people would not have things done to them or for them, whether by capitalists or bureaucrats, but one in which they would organise things for themselves.

The Coles are remembered for a lifetime of intellectual and practical activity on the thinking wing of the Labour Party and its associated institutions. For almost half a century it seemed that every ginger group or embryonic thinktank on the left bore the Cole imprint. They were the ubiquitous 'loyal grousers' or 'sensible extremists' (their own phrases) who were constantly prodding Labour to think more radically and act more boldly, although this was usually combined with a clear recognition of political realities. Not the least of the reasons why the Coles have something to say to us now is that they demonstrated the possibility of a kind of left-wing politics that avoided both uncritical loyalty and facile oppositionism. Like the Webbs, they believed in the importance of research and facts, as their vast output testifies, and the need to ground social theories in the tough soil of hard empirical evidence. Slogans, even good ones, were not enough.

So the Coles are writ large over the twentieth-century history of Labour and the left. Yet their really distinctive contribution to our own times remains that marriage of guild socialist argument with traditional Fabianism in the name of a 'new' Fabianism that was far more critical of the state and its bureaucratic dangers, and anxious to develop structures of social, economic and political governance that were designed to remove such dangers. No doubt the proposed structures were far too intricate and perhaps demanded too much participatory zeal, but the core vision is worth hanging on to. Certainly the Coles hung on to it, against the state tyranny of communism on one side and social democratic collectivism on the other. Towards the end of his life in the 1950s, at the close of his multi-volumed *A History of Socialist Thought*, GDH Cole still wanted to issue this personal credo: 'I am neither a communist nor a Social Democrat because I regard both as creeds of centralisation and bureaucracy, whereas I feel sure that a socialist society that is to be true to its equalitarian principles of human brotherhood must rest on the widest possible diffusion of power and responsibility, so as to enlist the active participation of as many as possible of its citizens in the tasks of democratic self-government.'

It is not surprising, then, that the 'participatory' left that appeared in the 1960s found the Coles' thought more interesting than much other social democratic fodder, nor that it continues to be revisited by those in search of theoretical ingredients and antecedents for a more self-governing kind of politics. At a time when there are lively arguments about the deficiencies of traditional forms of representation, attempts to reform the state and its services in ways designed to give a more direct say to users, and a dissatisfaction with top-down centralism, those old battles between the guild socialists and their Fabian adversaries take on a new relevance. They were exchanges of a high intellectual order, combining large theory with practical applications. We have need of both now. The Coles and the guild socialists asked many of the right questions, even if we are now required to provide our own answers.

7 | Harold Laski
Ellie Levenson

Isaac Kramnick and Barry Sheerman called Harold Laski 'everyone's favourite Socialist.' In fact, he was never everyone's favourite socialist. He was a prolific writer and thinker but his ideas, and his personality, attracted as much criticism as praise on both sides of the Atlantic. Nowadays he is rarely mentioned outside of Labour history groups and the obituaries of those he influenced. Yet he published prodigiously, producing thousands of articles and essays and over 20 books.

Laski's main contribution to political debate was the idea of pluralism and the recognition of the diverse allegiances people hold to many different authorities, not just the state. To Laski, America was the model of a pluralist society, with federalism and localism providing a series of checks and balances on the central state. His belief in the need to divide and devolve power is of special interest to the current devolution debate in the UK. The ideas behind the community activism debate that has seen the Government try to change the relationship between citizens and their public services, giving control to local communities and creating a 'public realm', also owe much to Laski.

In his vision of a pluralist society, Laski transferred some of the ideas and theories of eugenics to politics. He believed that, in order to compete with organisations such as trade unions and faith groups, the state had to be the strongest and the fittest institution, visibly serving the general good and not just the forces of capitalism. It therefore had to be buttressed with comprehensive information and sound evidence.

Laski's interest in eugenics may have dismayed later socialists, but in this pre-Nazi age it was shared by many other Fabians, particularly the Webbs and HG Wells. He was introduced to the subject by Frida Kerry, eight years his senior, whom he met at 16 and married two years later. Frida had studied medical gymnastics (physiotherapy) and was a passionate believer in eugenics, and Laski fell in love both with her and the subject. It provided the topic for his first published work, 'The Scope of Eugenics' published in the *Westminster Review* when he was only 17. To Laski, eugenics indicated that there were scientific solutions to social problems and contributed to his belief in birth control. At Oxford, he supported Fabian candidates to Union committees only if they were in favour of votes for women. In one piece of direct action he disrupted race week, a key event in the University social calendar, by hiring a boat and yelling 'votes for women' through a megaphone. He later planted a small bomb in Oxted, Surrey, in support of the cause. Laski was more an intellectual than a bombmaker however - the device failed to detonate properly, and from then on he concentrated on academic life rather than direct action.

This academic life began in North America, first in Canada then in the United States. Laski had his own special relationship with the United States. Though he hated America for the autonomy given to big business, he loved the pluralist nature of American society and the way power was dispersed through many bodies. He was able to separate the country from the administration. Meanwhile, he appreciated the need to look to Europe as well as America, asserting in *The Grammar of Politics* (1925) that a decision affecting France, for instance, must always be made in consultation with France. The League of Nations, which he encouraged, was not to Laski a super-sovereign state but an additional part of an international pluralist society bringing its own allegiances and ideas. Such argument surrounding the nature of the left's relationship with America and Europe is of course a significant political issue today. Meanwhile, the devolved UK assemblies find their feet and the Government pursues a programme of regional government in England.

Though he had some Fabian connections as a young man, Laski tended to think of the Fabians as statist. But in later life his antipathy to the state lessened and he came to believe that it had to take the lead in socialist reform. In *The Grammar of Politics*, he looked back on his previous beliefs and conceded that the state is a necessary co-ordinating unit, though he reaffirmed his belief that people should have as much autonomy as possible and that the state must allow each person to 'be his best self'. He shared with the Fabians a belief in democracy and the parliamentary process, and as Chair of the Fabian Society from 1946 to 48, he put great effort into its programme of research and publications. Yet some, including George Orwell, saw Laski's role as a public intellectual as wholly self-proclaimed. Laski saw Orwell as a man who failed to comprehend the economics behind socialism, while Orwell saw Laski as a bad writer who did not heed fact, calling him 'a socialist by allegiance and a liberal by temperament'.

The volume of his ideas and writings led to the 1930s being called 'the age of Laski' by one historian. His greatest personal achievements were as an intellectual and a teacher. He lectured not just at universities but also to workers around the country. As a co-opted member of the local council in Fulham in the mid 1930s (Frida was an elected member), he showed that his interest in localism was not just academic. He was heavily involved in library services, and was no intellectual snob, implementing a survey of users to find out the books they preferred (detective fiction) and ensuring that these books were ordered in. In a 1934 bid to bring power back to communities, Laski became a founder member of the National Council of Civil Liberties. It was during this period that his Marxism was at its height, though he faced a constant internal battle between Marxism and liberalism. He ran, with Victor Gollancz and John Strachey, the Left Book Club, which sought to unite the left; Gollancz declared that he had chosen Strachey for his sympathy with the Communist Party and Laski because of his membership of the Labour Party.

Laski's role as an intellectual was combined with his role as a Party man. Whilst his ideas challenged people's understanding of the state and their relationship to it, he was equally excited by the nitty gritty of Party life. He believed passionately in the Labour Party, serving on the National Executive Committee (NEC) from 1937 to 1945 and as Party Chairman in the election year of 1945-46. He absorbed himself in the internal workings of the party, delighting in small changes of policy here and there. But he also took advantage of his position to make controversial public statements. He frequently made the headlines, portrayed by the media as a sinister force pulling the strings behind the scenes. He called on the Labour leadership in 1945 to attend the Potsdam talks only as an observer, a demand immediately rejected by Attlee, who grew so exasperated by Laski's interventions that he finally admonished him: 'a period of silence on your part would be welcome.'

The following year, several newspapers reported that Laski had advocated violence to achieve social change had Labour not won the election. Laski issued libel writs against these publications, claiming that he had always, except for his brief flirtation with bombmaking as a student, had a commitment to parliamentary socialism, but he lost the case. Though his offers to resign from the LSE and the Party's NEC were rejected, and his costs were met through contributions from supporters at home and in America, Laski never really recovered his *joie de vivre*.

Laski's pluralism and his internationalism are major contributions to today's political world, but his main legacy to the Labour Party was his attitude towards politics. He was a networker who attacked the privileged whilst socialising with them - though it is often said that he exaggerated both his achievements and his acquaintances. Though criticised for it in his time, his networking and his ability to mix with all kinds of people, to know his enemy and to understand what will make people vote for a party which is not their natural home, are necessary political skills, and ones which led to the election of New Labour in 1997. Combining this pragmatism with intellectual vigour was a rare gift.

8 | Michael Young 1915-2002
Phillip Whitehead

No one was more happily named than Michael Young. One of the last times I saw him was in Pall Mall, on the way to a valedictory party for a former Fabian General Secretary who was Young's junior by some 15 years. Young overtook us, talking as fast as he walked in that allusive way he had. He overtook most people, often by the inside track, always eager to share 'the future, as it moves backwards into the continuing present.' At his memorial service the offspring of his three consecutive families combined to demonstrate his personal creativity. In his youth his mentors had taken him to breakfast with Franklin D. Roosevelt, and he had that great Democrat's ability for the telling phrase and the transformed idea. Very early on he understood that the delivery of the idea needed the pellucid simplicity of a tabloid opinion piece - but used to enable, not to destroy. The 1945 Labour manifesto became a celebrated example. 'Whatever you do, keep sentences short' he told the young David Miliband, on the eve of another Labour manifesto more than half a century later.

He always wanted to move on, to see ideas tested, sometimes to destruction. It could be exasperating for those left behind to administer the structures he conceived. The protégé of one year could come to believe that he was the pariah of the next. But Young asked no more in self-examination than he demanded of himself. The classic trinity of health, education and welfare would always need the dissenting voice from the orthodoxy of the day; it would be corrective, not corrosive. If the nation was wasting its talent or failing in its duty of care, the answer must always be one that acknowledged the human scale of the intended beneficiaries of change. As Hilary Perraton put it in a Churchill College lecture on Young's contribution to educational reform, he 'did not like the formal institutions of higher education, even while he was trying to widen access to them.' The in-house inspiration of the Plowden Committee, the man with privileged access to (and the lifelong friendship of) Anthony Crosland came to worry about elites of merit and their likely impact. My generation, the first of our kind to arrive at university through the grammar schools and generous state provision, were stunned by *The Rise of The Meritocracy*. This dystopian projection of our future set us wondering. That tattered 1961 paperback is one of the few books I've kept for the emotions it provoked - and still does when early predictive school-testing and the fervent promotion of deserving elites have pushed aside equality of outcome as 'pre-merit thinking.'

Of course we are still far away from complete social mobility and its consequence that 'the least responsible jobs should be filled by the least able people.' We need more Sure Start, not less, more public provision to reduce disadvantaged access. What Young was able to demonstrate, early and often, was that there are many ways to do this, which rely on pluralism, diversity and fraternity as the solvents of the acquisitive inequality of our current society. The National Extension College was the precursor of the Open University, the Open College for the Arts, and a revolution in distance learning around the globe. The technical abundance of the modern mass media gives us today a wider 'world without walls' than was possible when Young proposed it on that heady day in 1972 when the Open University began. His advice would be simple: overtake the problem before it overtakes us. We need Young's flair in the age of the website trafficker and the monopolists of intellectual property alike. We need his mordant commentary on a world in which much that we should be able to access is under remote control, and we may be, literally, patented out of our own skins.

Some market forces have made 'consumerism' a pejorative term for exploitation. Young appreciated the irony of that. He had begun at the point of empowerment, baulking at Labour's dependence on the Morrisonian corporations and the trade union dominated producer hegemony. While still at Transport House he had begun to respond to the pressure for intelligent consumer advice and product evaluation from former colleagues at Political and Economic Planning (PEP), who already had the model of the American Consumers Union. The group which he helped to set up alongside the Institute for Community Studies in Bethnal Green - the original *garagiste tendence* - launched a magazine - *Which?* - that became, as Young recalled in 1990, the most immediate success he had ever had. He was, albeit briefly, its first director with Eirlys Roberts as the editor of the magazine. Consumers' Association came to have more than a million members. Self-financing, independent of both government and business, it was a power to be reckoned with. How should that power be harnessed? In 1960, a year after *The Rise of The Meritocracy*, Young opened a second front. *The Chipped White Cups of Dover* went so far as to see a progressive consumers' party as an alternative to Labour. The Fabian Society refused to publish it, and he went elsewhere. The idea had not found its time and when he returned as chairman of a new National Consumer Council set up in 1975, which remains to this day in a somewhat uneasy relationship with the CA, Michael saw it as the start of a new troika with the TUC and the CBI opening up the old corporate dualities. It did not work out quite like that and within a few years he had found a new third force which, for a while, enthused him: the SDP - politics on merit. When he came to debate with us at the Fabian New School of 1984 he was less concerned to convert us than to replace us with a rebranded alternative, the Tawney Society. It planted an egalitarian flag on our cherished ground, but not for long. Now, 20 years on, everyone has rediscovered Tawney, but no one remembers the Tawney Society. Young himself slipped quietly back into the ranks of the Labour peers.

The point, though, is that he was always open to the case for change, inventing institutions which would survive if they could be passed into capable hands to meet a palpable need. The debates about consumerism never resolved whether it is better to have an independently-funded and freestanding presence in a commercial world, or to have state funding and its potential constraints. Both have survived, and so has the global organisation (now the Consumer Congress) which he did much to inspire. The consumer as citizen, not the consumer as acquirer, remains an inspiration. We know what Young would tell us today, and not only because he survived into this century. At the millennium he returned in *Equality and Public Service* to that manifesto of 55 years before, and to the guiding principles of equity in the distribution of incomes and the importance of public service. How was it that inequality was increasing, and public service disparaged? He conceded that 'something has been done, and more is promised, to raise the bottom, hit very little at the top .... poverty is not a taboo word but equality is, and redistribution nearly so.' Whereas his meritocrats rewarded themselves in perks which distorted national equality of income, the executive rich of the 21st century wanted it all. Young lamented that it has become 'a new golden age, not for equality but for booty.'

The lesson for us is that without a sense of social responsibility, and the tax framework to underpin it, we are into the politics of pillage. The private sector offers partnership in return for exemption. The casualties - pensioners, users of marginal public services, supporters of mutual enterprise - can be pushed aside. Debates about choice, so much in vogue, are vacuous for the choiceless. Young was a lamplighter. He saw these things, from a distance learning experiment in Colombia or Mauritius, family education, health care as fraternity, from the families observed in East London whose varied needs and talents mirrored his own. The constant for him, as it should be for us, was community, in the line that passes through Tawney, Halsey, Hutton and the rest, but is forever Young.

9 | Anthony Crosland 1918-1977
Austin Mitchell

Labour's long history abounds with attempts to define what we're about, but Tony Crosland's *The Future of Socialism*, published half a century ago, is the most powerful and the only one still relevant today. Though he died quarter of a century ago Crosland's body is still wrestled over by those who claim he would have supported the SDP, the EU, the Third Way, Blairism or Brownism.

The message endures because Crosland adjusted socialism to the new age we still live in. Before that, socialism, born of Marxism, looked to the state to take on the power of capitalism, to build the platform of welfare and benefits, to break the power of privilege and to run businesses for public benefit not private profit. The great Labour Government of 1945-51 used state powers, mobilised for war, to build a post-war settlement of nationalised utilities, welfare state, higher public spending and Keynesian demand management for full employment. On these foundations the affluent society, and the mixed economy, were built.

Crosland's achievement was to abandon socialist fundamentalism, jettison ideology and drop what no longer fitted in the new world: state control, nationalisation, redistribution by expropriation, equality by levelling down rather than up, and all the easy slogans which had been the staple rhetoric of the past but had never been thought through. They were becoming unsaleable as the nation reacted against war-time controls, the private sector powered ahead and new dynamics of competition, markets, choice and consumption became more important.

As AJP Taylor said, 'Few even sang "England Arise". England had risen all the same.' We were better off, and with the basic problems tackled, socialism had to change. Crosland set us out on a new march to new goals, defining socialism as ends not means, and certainly not a rigid ideology, nationalisation or state power. Its goal is the betterment of the mass of the people in a more equal, fairer society. Whatever builds that is socialist.

Which made growth central. Rather than arguing about fairer shares of a constant cake the aim should be to grow the cake. Growth makes redistribution less painful, creates the surplus for it via public spending, and enthrones altruism. Growth does more than the state to improve the lot of the people and to finance the education, the welfare, the opportunities and the betterment all deserve.

'I have never', said Crosland, 'been able to see why high consumption and brotherly love should be thought incompatible - why should not the brothers be affluent and the love conducted under conditions of reasonable comfort?'

No-one could really argue against such a commitment though subsequent Labour Governments haven't excelled at achieving it, partly because of caution, partly because other priorities, such as the exchange rate, 'defeating inflation' or 'stability' have intruded. Yet the main hostility to Crosland's priorities came from elitists: those who know better than the people what the people want, and from snobby, middle-class feelings that the working-class didn't deserve better houses for their whippets and pigeons, or baths in which to store their coal. This produced a chorus of fears that growth would encourage materialism, greed and selfishness - possibly even make the workers Conservative. It would 'spoil' the working class, ruin the environment, deplete the world's resources, lower standards in education ('more means worse'). It all looks laughable now though 'standards' are still assumed in Britain to be a middle-class preserve.

Everything flowed from the emphasis on growth. Capitalism would advance the cause by generating growth, provided it was encouraged to invest more and distribute less. Competition was good and though ownership mattered less Crosland saw no reason why the state should not compete either by introducing public competitors in underperforming sectors, or by providing risk capital, breaking bottlenecks and encouraging investment. Regulation became more important than physical controls or direction. Thus the mixed, not the socialist, economy was to build the base on which the better society could rest. It was to generate rising surpluses for social spending and a national superannuation scheme and to expand industrial democracy by bringing unions and workers into consultation.

This good society owes more to American than Soviet influences and Crosland's prescription influenced, rather than shaped, the Labour Governments of the 1960s and 1970s. It allowed them to go on, as he urged, to tackle the issues of wellbeing which are not specifically socialist, such as freedom of personal and leisure life, divorce reform, tolerance, higher cultural values, and a more colourful, civilised and 'gay' life for all, freed from the smug censoriousness of the ideologues, even the dull and dutiful Fabians. The privileged middle-class world Crosland had known was to be available to all.

Crosland's analysis is still relevant. He grapples with the questions which still preoccupy us and the problems which still plague us, in each case suggesting the approach (greater use of fiscal than monetary management, more emphasis on industry, production and jobs than finance and speculation) rather than prescribing the solution. Failures since result not from his prescriptions but from our reluctance to follow them. Other fashions - democratic socialism, stakeholder communitarism, the third way - have intruded. We've distracted ourselves by multi-cause peddling of feminism, ethnic politics, environmentalism, animal rights, anti-war, anti-GM and anti-nuclear. We've lost sight of the basic need to run the economy for growth and production.

Yet now as we recover from the decades of failure and economic masochism, and the realisation grows that sectional causes can only succeed if Labour generates the growth to boost redistribution and public spending, Crosland's prescription re-emerges. The failures of the market and laissez faire attitudes bring us back to 'reinventing government', to regulating the excesses of capitalism and to furthering equality. In the end Labour still stands or falls by its success in generating economic growth to achieve its priorities of equality, fairness, better public spending and enhanced welfare.

In 1956 I thought *The Future of Socialism* the most exciting political prescription I'd ever read. Today it doesn't seem as original and exciting as it did. Yet it's still both relevant and enduring, because it distils what we as a party, and as Fabians, are about: a party dedicated to building a better world for the majority by putting the people first. Call them the 'working class', the 'real people', or, as Crosland called them from 1959, Grimbarians, the constituents he took as his touchstone of reality, Labour is essentially about improving their lot. If we've not done that as fully, or as richly, as they deserve it's because we failed, not because Crosland was wrong.

10 | Brian Abel-Smith 1926-1996
Peter Townsend

Brian Abel-Smith is someone whose value to Britain - and to Labour Governments, past and future - needs greater recognition. He did more than anyone else to consolidate the NHS in its early years, when in 1951 it came under threat from the incoming Tory Government of being emasculated and even dismantled. He was the key figure in the eventual adoption during the 1970s by Britain of earnings-related top-up state pensions and much else in social security. His self-effacing work for the World Health Organisation for 40 years in 62 countries until his death in 1996 to establish good health services was extraordinary and is unlikely to be matched by anyone again. These three things show what he would be saying today. He was one of the giants of international and national social welfare of the twentieth century.

His origins and balance of skills are the stuff of open-mouthed wonder. Born in 1926, the younger son of Brigadier-General Lionel Abel-Smith and therefore, so it was said, 27th in line to the throne, he saw military service in the final years of the war and became ADC to the military governor of the British zone in Austria during 1947-8.

Despite this top-drawer start in life he did not deviate from thoroughgoing democratic socialism. Aside from being a constant source of Fabian Society initiatives and management (being elected - for several years top of the poll - executive member, Treasurer, Chairman and Vice-President), strenuous efforts were made to get him into Parliament. Hugh Dalton, a post-war Chancellor of the Exchequer, wanted him to follow in his footsteps into a rock-solid Durham Labour constituency. He was judged by Dalton and Tony Crosland as well as Harold Wilson to be a likely Minister, even a Chancellor of the Exchequer, in a future Labour Government. Instead, Abel-Smith decided in the mid-1950s to remain in the political back room.

That room became a power house of directed energy. After Labour returned to power in 1964, Richard Crossman, Barbara Castle, David Ennals and Peter Shore tempted him in turn to be their top adviser. He worked with them (and part-time at LSE) from 1968 to 1979. He wrote terse, immaculate briefs. Barbara Castle once said she had made the two best adviser appointments - Jack Straw for his low cunning and Brian Abel-Smith for his brains. Certainly as senior adviser Abel-Smith won unqualified, and uniquely rare, respect from senior civil servants.

Distilled clarity is the mark of all his writing. In 1953, aged 25, he published his first Fabian pamphlet, *The Reform of Social Security*. He said that the crisis in social security was political rather than economic 'and the Labour Party must be on its guard against reactionary plans for "reform". ... Raising benefits as of right up to the level of those subject to a means test would remove much real distress and save the expensive process of supplementation.' He was keen to argue the economic benefits of universal entitlement - low-cost administration, increased public saving, practicability, consumer satisfaction, economic growth and constraint on market excess. This gave an edge of advantage to the multiple social benefits that many people recognised in such entitlement.

Today he would be arguing for the extension of human rights and for more elaborate public service as a necessary sheet anchor for the global market. He used the rapier rather than the cutlass to assault extreme individual wealth as well as unrestrained business power.

He wrote often about redistribution as a social good. In a final article, published by LSE after his death in 1996, aged 69, he said that the growth of poverty in Britain, especially child poverty, was inexcusable. Nonetheless, 'the sorrows of Britain in the 1990s are as nothing compared with the fate of Africa. While the OECD countries throw aid at them, at the same time they close many of their markets, take their debt repayments and interest on a scale greater than the aid they give and rival each other in exploiting the vast world market for armaments.' There had to be 'debt forgiveness' at the heart of real development.

As an instrument of redistribution he always believed social insurance had to be given priority - in poor countries as much as in those rich countries with elaborate systems requiring improvement. Compared with general taxation there were particular advantages, of pooling risks, identifying individual benefits, establishing solidarity across generations, social groups and classes and guaranteeing national savings - which provide sharp meaning to 'universality'.

In the mid 1950s the looming divide on pensions was provoking national concern. This was forestalled by the Labour leader, Hugh Gaitskell, and Richard Crossman appointing Richard Titmuss, Brian and myself - a trio described by a Tory Minister of Pensions as the Labour Party's 'skiffle group' - to prepare a new plan for national superannuation. The plan drew on a joint Fabian pamphlet of 1955 by Brian and myself. Its recommendations were endorsed at the Party's annual conference in October 1957. Once Labour was re-elected the scheme went through various hoops, and a Bill, confirming the 'State Earnings-Related Pension Scheme' (SERPS) was enacted in 1975. Abel-Smith was the key figure who persuaded Crosland and Gaitskell, and then Wilson, of its viability, and he also saw the project through to fruition with Crossman in the late 1960s and with Castle in the mid 1970s.

Today he would be arguing that something like that scheme had to be introduced in the next phase of Labour government, along with greatly increased universal child benefit, as the necessary foundation for successful social policy in the Labour attack from 1997 on poverty. That attack would incorporate an earnings-related top-up and a much increased basic State pension. Stakeholder pensions would go; Pension Credit would be drastically scaled down and later withdrawn. Private pensions would have to meet stronger public rules of accountability.

Abel-Smith would be deeply sceptical, at a time when incomes are becoming rapidly more unequal, of the intention expressed by Labour at the end of the 1990s to shift the cost of pensions from 40:60 to 60:40 in favour of private provision. Like Richard Titmuss, who was scornful of the social pretensions of the insurance industry in his Fabian pamphlet *The Irresponsible Society*, he would be arguing for a big public scheme for universal social security, alongside the minimum wage, to represent a civilised and collectively organised minimum living standard for all, and also act as a model for private and voluntary schemes to emulate and complement.

Health was Abel-Smith's even larger objective. His first major work on the cost of the NHS was already in active preparation as a PhD at Cambridge when Titmuss invited him to work jointly with him to influence policy. A government committee - the Guillebaud Committee - had been set up to investigate the cost of the new service, alleged to be rising out of control. Abel-Smith went on the attack, demonstrating that, far from rising, the total cost was declining proportionate to GNP. Even to maintain the 1949 rate would involve £67million extra commitment.

Abel-Smith's analysis was typically thorough and well-argued and neither the Committee nor the Tory Government was able to make a case for new or higher charges. At a stroke the newly-introduced NHS attracted all-party endorsement. Together he and Titmuss spent the next ten years resolutely demolishing the frantic arguments for private care from DS Lees, Arthur Seldon, John Jewkes and others.

The text of the book derived from Abel-Smith's PhD was extensively quoted by the Guillebaud Committee before its publication in 1955, when he became Assistant Lecturer at the LSE - one of Timuss's so-called 'Titmice'. By the early 1960s, after rapid promotion, he was advising governments on what might be learned from 15 years experience of the NHS. To Canadians in 1965 he said 'there is a danger ... in assuming that the only purpose in establishing a comprehensive and universal health programme is to remove the financial barrier to personal health care.' This was not the only deserved achievement of the NHS. 'Much more important was the creation of a framework within which the quality of medical care could be improved faster than could be expected to occur in a private market.' He struggled to define this framework in many of the 25 books and 98 papers and articles he published on health. It certainly meant democratic public control, long term planning of health services and, as testified in his superb histories of nurses, hospitals and doctors (1960-1964), accountability of the principal health care professions to elected politicians and not just to their professional peers. After the Thatcher years, he showed in *An Introduction to Health* that in the rich countries with neo-liberal policies this was becoming a bit like trying to square the circle. In developing countries the direction that policy should take remained more straightforward. User charges, as he showed for Tanzania in 1992, could be heavily criticised. Compulsory health insurance remained the only advisable course of action to fulfil rights to health care treatment.

Brian Abel-Smith deserves legendary status alongside Titmuss. He was the power behind the throne. He was at the time a more flexible exponent of new ideas in social policy and an ingenious economist. To the well-honed and memorable text of Titmuss he added political judgment and economic authority. After the death of Titmuss in 1973, he played a powerful role in developing international health services for 23 more years. This role came in part from his insights into the law. He was co-author of two major books calling for a root-and-branch overhaul of the legal profession and organisation. More than anyone I remember he helped well-evidenced reason to prevail over the conventional wisdom.

11 | John P. Mackintosh 1929-1978
Greg Rosen

There are few essays on Labour's political thought that do not acknowledge the seminal role of Anthony Crosland's *The Future of Socialism* and in the next breath bemoan the failure of either Crosland or a younger generation of social democrats to produce a worthy sequel. If anyone was to have done it, it is likely that it would have been John P. Mackintosh, who was planning to do so when his death from a heart tumour, aged only 48, robbed him of the opportunity. Mackintosh was a unique and celebrated thinker, polemicist and parliamentarian. Though never, due to his combination of mischievous wit and an impolitic devotion to causes, made a minister, his achievements remain more tangible than those of many who were. Born in 1929, he was already a distinguished academic, the first Professor of Politics at Strathclyde University, on his election in 1966 as Labour MP for Berwick and East Lothian. His groundbreaking analysis of post-Bagehot 'prime-ministerial' government, *The British Cabinet*, had already been published in 1962. He was, with Enoch Powell, Michael Foot and Brian Walden, one of the four most commanding parliamentary orators of his era. He was a prolific writer, securing regular columns in both the *Times* and the *Scotsman*, and became an accomplished broadcaster. Such was his seemingly boundless energy that in the final year of his life he combined his duties as MP with those of Professor of Politics at Edinburgh University. Despite his early death in July 1978, his legacy as a thinker still shines brightly today.

Entering Parliament a revisionist social-democrat, in little more than a year he had stolen the headlines on the eve of Labour's 1967 conference with his pamphlet *Change Gear! Towards a Socialist Strategy*, co-written with MPs David Marquand and David Owen. It was Mackintosh who set the pace. For Owen, Mackintosh was 'the person who most contributed most to my ideas.' For Marquand, Mackintosh was his political 'elder brother.' Some of the measures he called for, such as devaluation, the creation of the DHSS, wider legal safeguards against racial discrimination and the establishment of parliamentary select committees, the Wilson government was later to implement or pilot. Others, such as the televising of Parliament, came later. 30 years on, devolution, a minimum wage, the establishment of 'education priority areas', road pricing and welfare reform became key planks of New Labour policy.

Mackintosh's causes ranged widely. His pioneering campaigns for more liberal and civilised drinking laws foreshadowed New Labour's reform of England's restrictive and antiquated licensing law. He was an early and, complained Barbara Castle, 'unscrupulously brilliant' advocate of Britain's involvement in what was then the EEC.

Even before Callaghan's famous Ruskin speech, it was Mackintosh who sought to point out that the great debates about school structures had been conducted almost to the exclusion of the issue of school standards, and that the progressive reaction against traditional, more didactic teaching methods had gone too far. In an article for the *Scotsman* in 1976 he wrote: 'In front of me I have *Mathematics for Schools* by Fletcher and Howell, and its ingenuity in helping the non-numerate to visualise numerical relationships is impressive. But one has to witness the acute frustration of the numerate child (aged 7-13 for this book) having to draw five blue cars and the three red cars to establish that 5-3 equals 2.' Two years later in the *Political Quarterly* he asked: 'Does equality mean that within one comprehensive school there should be no streaming according to ability or even no examinations? If so, does there come a point where the lack of any indicators of ability or effort militates against the working class child with no connections?'

Mackintosh was perhaps the Commons' most tenacious campaigner for a proper system of parliamentary select committees. So much so was he the parliamentarian that, as his friend and parliamentary colleague Dickson Mabon observed at Mackintosh's memorial service, the P in his name could easily have stood for 'Parliament'. It was Mackintosh who encouraged Richard Crossman's experimental select committees during the late 1960s. And when these were snuffed out after Crossman's retirement from government, Mackintosh took to the airwaves, persuading Granada Television to stage a series of mock debates to popularise his argument that MPs were 'too ignorant to do their job' without a proper system of select committees.

It is probably for his campaign to restore a Scottish Parliament that Mackintosh is held in highest esteem today. As Gordon Brown has remarked, it was Mackintosh who kept the flame of Labour's commitment to devolution alive during Willie Ross's dour stewardship of the Scottish Office. Mackintosh explained the rise of the SNP in the late 1960s and early 1970s in terms of a dual Scottish-British consciousness: 'With a dual identity, there is a simple alternative if the pride in being British wanes: just be Scottish.' The argument continues to underpin the Scottish Labour Party's belief that the Scottish people want a parliament but not independence, regarding themselves as both Scottish and British, and indeed also European. Mackintosh believed that only a period of successful Westminster government, rebuilding pride in Britain, could reverse the march of the SNP. It is a prescription, as New Labour strategist and MP Douglas Alexander wrote in the *Scotsman* of 17 August 1998, 'that holds true today'. Such was his public stature during the 1970s that Tam Dalyell and many others remain convinced that had Mackintosh lived, the 1979 devolution referendum would have led to the creation of a Scottish Assembly. Even now, 35 years after the publication of his seminal *Devolution of Power* in 1968, it is Mackintosh's formulation of the intellectual case for devolution that underpins Labour's creation of the Scottish Parliament and the Welsh Assembly.

For Mackintosh, given that the Civil Service bureaucracy which ran Scotland had already been devolved to St Andrew's House in Edinburgh, 'the case for devolution is the case for democratic control of the machine.' His answer to the infamous West Lothian question, posed by his friend Tam Dalyell, is still cited in Parliament in defence of devolution today. Mackintosh argued that the question - which asked why Scottish MPs should make laws affecting only English constituencies when English MPs would no longer be able to legislate on issues devolved to the Scottish Parliament - was underpinned by a 'complete myth about Parliament'. Citing Mackintosh's writings, Douglas Alexander explained to the Commons in 1999: 'Mackintosh's critique rested on the observation, which still holds true today, that in the majority of cases, the legislation affecting, for example, education in West Bromwich is initiated not by individual members of the House, Scottish or otherwise, but by the Executive.'

Perhaps most fundamentally, however, Mackintosh sought to modernise social democracy itself. Although he was to die before he could produce a systematic synthesis of his political ideas in book form, his critiques of the inadequacies of revisionism were as incisive as they were wide-ranging. He had yet to formulate all the answers but he nevertheless asked the questions. He remained entirely committed to the goal of full employment and rejected unequivocally the panaceas of the monetarist right: 'It was one thing in the nineteenth century to allow the immutable laws of economics to create mass unemployment, it is another to do so deliberately to meet right-wing economists' distaste for the laborious and tricky task of negotiating and enforcing sensible wages policy.' However, the same article sought to explore a growing and persistent theme: that Crosland's position was fundamentally flawed by the absence of any rationale for the existence of a thriving private sector within the mixed economy it professed to advocate: 'the building of a social atmosphere which regards profit as sordid and

48

which suspects private enterprise has, over time, weakened and demoralised the private sector to the extent that it no longer provides the necessary growth to keep the whole economy moving.' Writing in the *Scotsman* in 1978, he attacked a 'basic error' of Croslandism in talking 'endlessly about the distribution of wealth, its taxation and use for this and that but very little about the creation of wealth ... the central task of justifying and producing a thriving mixed economy remains.' 25 years later, that task is central to New Labour.

12 | Bernard Crick 1929-
Andrew Gamble

Bernard Crick has much to teach us through his writing but also through his practical example. Like so many Fabians he has combined intellectual reflection and analysis with attempts to put ideas into practice. Recognised as one of the great political essayists of his generation, he has always been concerned in his writing to address the general reader and the active citizen. To this end he became one of the longest serving editors of the *Political Quarterly* and in the 1990s launched the Orwell Prize to encourage the best political writing. He has held academic posts at the LSE, Sheffield and Birkbeck College, University of London, and has written many influential academic books on politics, democracy, the reform of Parliament, national identity, and citizenship. He has attracted most attention for his first book *In Defence of Politics*, and for his later biography, *George Orwell: A Life*.

Never content to be a conventional scholar (he is deeply out of sympathy with the modern university), and describing himself as a life-long gadfly, he has always been deeply committed to the cause of political education and of active citizenship. He has helped launch many new institutions such as the Politics Association for teachers of politics in schools, the Study of Parliament Group and the Association for Citizenship Teaching. His unique talents were recognised by David Blunkett when he appointed him to chair the advisory group on the Teaching of Citizenship and Democracy in Schools in 1997. The report of this group was widely welcomed and Crick was asked to oversee its implementation. Further public commissions have followed. He was asked to advise on citizenship tests and is currently Adviser on Active Citizenship to the Home Office.

What he has to say to us now is in one sense what he has always been saying to us, although we are more ready to hear it because political apathy and disengagement are on the rise, and the need for a revival of democratic citizenship is widely recognised. However, Crick's message is not an easy one to digest. When *In Defence of Politics* was first published in 1962, Edward Shils praised its sobriety, liberal spirit, and toughness of mind, while Isaiah Berlin called it exceedingly clever but also disturbing, penetrating and serious. In that book, Crick defended politics as the only way of holding a free society together, and sought to dispel illusions as to what politics involved. Since a conflict of interests is inevitable in any state, the processes and institutions of politics are required in order to find out what those interests are, and to show citizens the impossibility of all interests being satisfied simultaneously, and therefore the necessity of negotiation and compromise if social order, pluralism, diversity and freedom are to be sustained. Crick's point is that it is impossible to determine what the public interest is without trying to find out what it is that people want, and how the different things that they want can be reconciled. Only politics can do this. This means that democratic politics will often be scorned by many on left, right and centre because it is messy, unprincipled, approximate, and because politicians so often appear devious, evasive and untrustworthy. They never measure up to expectations. Crick's hard point is that they never will, and in expecting them to do so, we find ourselves perpetually disillusioned, which is why so many people disengage from politics altogether, seeking comfort elsewhere.

Crick does not believe democracy will ever be attractive, in the sense that government will be conducted by individuals of high principle who only act in the public interest and for the public good. They could only do so if the conflict of interests arising from a diverse society was suppressed and the public good imposed. This does not mean, however, that Crick thinks that democracy should be populist. Some of his strongest writing has been against the trivialisation and dumbing down of citizens by the modern media, a process which he argues Orwell satirised in *Nineteen Eighty-Four*. The state of depoliticised cultural debasement in which the proles are kept was a Swiftian satire on the British popular press of Orwell's day. Crick has reflected ruefully on what has happened since that time, and on the use of one of Orwell's most famous images, Big Brother, as the name for the reality TV programme which embodies that cultural debasement most clearly. The power of the media has greatly increased, while that of the structures of democratic participation have sharply diminished since Orwell's time. In Crick's view the structures that can preserve an open and pluralist democracy have continually to be fought for, otherwise they can all too easily be lost.

This is his passion for citizenship - to replace the 'empty mob' and the 'hate-filled mob', to which so much of the modern media, in alliance with some politicians, seeks to reduce citizens. Crick argued for citizenship to be included in the national curriculum as a necessary requirement for a democratic society, if not a sufficient one. The strengthening of democracy through the creation of a citizen culture rather than a subject culture, and the encouragement of citizens to be active, to argue, to discuss, above all to participate in whatever political forms are available to express their interests and their hopes: this for Crick is the process of political education itself, which is never ending. His idea of politics in the national curriculum is not to confine it to the teaching of civics, the nuts and bolts of how government works, but to enable participation in politics itself.

Crick has always had fierce views about most political subjects, from the Falklands and Iraq to Northern Ireland and presidentialism. His view of politics does not mean that people should seek a watered down consensus. He likes quoting Ernest Gellner: 'socially tolerant always, intellectually tolerant never'. He maintains that no progress of any kind is possible without political argument, political education and political participation, and that to achieve these the political class has to stop talking to itself and engage with citizens, however uncomfortable and messy and less than ideal that may often turn out to be.

About the Authors

Robin Cook is Labour MP for Livingston. He was Secretary of State for Foreign and Commonwealth Affairs from 1997 to 2001 and Leader of the House of Commons from 2001 until his resignation from the cabinet in 2003. His most recent book is *The Point of Departure*, an account of the build-up to and the consequences of the second gulf war, as well as a broader look at the Blair Government since its re-election in 2001. He was a member of the Fabian Society Executive for many years and was Chair in 1990-91.

Andrew Gamble is Professor of Politics at the University of Sheffield and joint editor of the *Political Quarterly*. His publications include *The Free Economy and the Strong State: Politics of Thatcherism; Hayek: The Iron Cage of Liberty; Politics and Fate;* and *Between Europe and America: The Future of British Politics.*

Roy Hattersley was MP for Birmingham Sparkbrook from 1964 to 1997 and Deputy Leader of the Labour Party from 1983 to 1992. He served as a government minister in a wide range of departments, becoming Secretary of State for Prices and Consumer Protection in 1976, as well as holding a number of senior shadow portfolios. He is a prolific author, having published numerous academic texts, biographies, collections of essays and novels as well as regular newspaper columns.

Sunder Katwala has been General Secretary of the Fabian Society since October 2003. Prior to this he was a leader writer and internet editor at the *Observer* and founding Research Director of the Foreign Policy Centre.

Yasmin Khan is completing a PhD in Modern History at St Antony's College, Oxford. Her next project will be a biography of Annie Besant.

Ellie Levenson was editor of the *Fabian Review* from 2002 to 2004. She has had work published in the *New Statesman*, the *Guardian*, the *Observer* and the *Independent*.

Guy Lodge is a member of the Fabian Society Executive and a former Chair of the Young Fabians. He co-edited the Fabian pamphlet *Radicals and Reformers: A Century of Fabian Thought* (2000). He works at the Constitution Unit, School of Public Policy, University College, London.

Austin Mitchell has been Labour MP for Grimsby since 1977, when he was selected after a career as a political science lecturer at Oxford and in New Zealand, and as a broadcaster and journalist with the BBC and Yorkshire Television. He has written numerous publications on the Labour Party and wider politics, while also managing to produce a considerable number of articles for various journals and newspapers. He joined the Fabian Society in 1961 from New Zealand and has been a member ever since. A former Chair of the Society, he is currently on the Fabian Executive.

Raymond Plant is Professor of Jurisprudence and Political Philosophy at King's College London Law School and is a Labour member of the House of Lords. He was made a peer in 1992 and until 1996 was a spokesperson on Home Affairs. He has been Professor of European Political Thought at the University of Southampton and Master of St Catherine's College, Oxford. He is the author of several Fabian pamphlets, including *Equality, Markets and the State*, published in 1983.

Greg Rosen is Chair of the Labour History Group and editor of the *Dictionary of Labour Biography*. His forthcoming book *I'm Telling You and You'll Listen!* is a history of the Labour Party incorporating the great speeches which tell the story of the dreams that inspired it and the battles that divided it. A former adviser at the Home Office and at the Amalgamated Engineering and Electrical Union (AEEU), he was first elected onto the Fabian Society Executive in 2000 and has served as Chair of the Fabian Research and Publications Committee since 2002.

Fabian Thinkers

Peter Townsend is Vice President of the Fabian Society. In his late twenties and early thirties he worked with Richard Titmuss and Brian Abel-Smith at the LSE, and together they produced a pensions plan adopted by Labour and finally enacted under the leadership of Barbara Castle in 1976. He was appointed to the new University of Essex as Professor of Sociology in 1963. He is responsible for books and research reports on poverty, inequalities in health, disability and ageing, and rejoined LSE as Professor of International Social Policy in 1998.

Phillip Whitehead is Labour MEP for the East Midlands. He was Chair of the Fabian Society in 1978 and Chair of the Consumers' Association from 1990 to 1994.

Tony Wright is Labour MP for Cannock Chase. He currently chairs the Public Administration Select Committee. He is co-editor of the *Political Quarterly*. In 2002 he became Chair of the newly established Centre for Public Scrutiny. He has also been Co-Chair of the Campaign for Freedom of Information, and Chair of the Fabian Society. His most recent publication is *A New Social Contract: From Targets to Rights in Public Services*, a pamphlet produced by the Fabians.